Hunter
in the *Snow*
The Lynx

SUSAN BONNERS

Little, Brown and Company

BOSTON   NEW YORK   TORONTO   LONDON

*This book is dedicated to those who have faced the blizzards and
followed the footprints in the snow to bring back the story of the lynx*

First Edition

With thanks to **J. David Brittell**, Washington State Department of Wildlife; **Rainer H. Brocke**, College of Environmental Science and Forestry, SUNY Syracuse; **Steve Contento and Lisa Zembek**, Ross Park Zoo, Binghamton, New York; **Jack Curtin and Linda Rohr**, Franklin Park Zoo, Boston; **Gregg Dancho**, Beardsley Zoo, Bridgeport, Connecticut; **Jacques Dancosse and Rachel Léger**, Biodôme de Montréal; **Carol Day, John Matuszek, Nancy Pajeau, and Jim Rowell**, Brookfield Zoo, Chicago; **William Garner and Brad Muir**, Prince Albert National Park, Saskatchewan; **Roger Hamel**, Coaticook, Québec; **Rich Hendron and Gina Phillips**, Utah's Hogle Zoo, Salt Lake City; **Nancy and Lew Hurxthal**, Plymouth, Massachusetts; **Lloyd B. Keith**, Department of Wildlife Ecology, University of Wisconsin; **Gary M. Koehler**, Hornocker Wildlife Research Institute, University of Idaho; **Clément Lanthier and Louise Sylvestre**, Société Zoologique de Granby, Québec; **Victor Miller**, Quetico Provincial Park, Ontario; **John Stoner**, Metropolitan Toronto Zoo; **Robert H. Sylar, Jr.**, Knoxville Zoo; and **Patricia J. Wynne**, New York City.

Library of Congress Cataloging-in-Publication Data

Bonners, Susan.
    Hunter in the snow : the lynx / Susan Bonners. — 1st ed.
        p.   cm.
    Summary: Focuses on a year in the life of a female lynx,
describing hunting practices, courtship and mating, denning, and the
birth and care of the young.
    ISBN 0-316-10201-6
    1. Lynx — Juvenile literature.   [1. Lynx.] I. Title. II. Title:
Lynx.
QL737.C23B65 1994
599.74'428 — dc20   93-24975

10 9 8 7 6 5 4 3 2 1

SC

Published simultaneously in Canada by Little, Brown & Company
(Canada) Limited

Printed in Hong Kong

The artwork for this book was done with pastels,
both pencils and sticks, on Stonehenge paper.

All night and into the morning, a snowstorm has blown through the forest. Bedded under a rock ledge, a Canada lynx watches the last snowflakes sift down. With the fall of twilight on this late-December afternoon, the time has come to hunt.

Her paws brushing through the fluffy new layer of white, the lynx pads lightly on the crust of the winter snowpack. Many other animals would break through the crust, exhausting themselves with every step, but not the lynx. Her large feet, thickly furred even on the undersides, spread out her weight like snowshoes. Retracted within the furry snowshoes are inch-long claws.

She picks her way with ease through the tangle of fallen branches and rotting logs, instinctively staying hidden in dense cover. She will not reveal herself by crossing a large clearing. Sometimes she leaps, as if for the joy of it, her long back legs thrusting her body forward.

Wherever she can, she walks on downed tree trunks to raise herself higher so that she can see farther into the forest. Keen night vision, aided by sensitive hearing, will lead her to prey. The tufts on her ears may help collect sound.

She moves quickly through this stand of hundred-year-old white spruce. She will not find her prey here. She hunts a plant-eating animal that would find little food in this part of the forest: the lowest edible branches of the trees are overhead, far out of the reach of most plant eaters. The low-growing shrubs are covered by snow.

Instead the lynx goes to a part of her territory that was destroyed by fire twenty years ago. After the fire, only stumps were left on the blackened earth, but soon, new shoots poked up. Now young trees grow there, half-buried in the snow. The lower branches of aspen and birch are in easy reach of the snowshoe hare, the lynx's favorite prey. Small evergreens provide the hare with shelter from the biting cold.

When she nears this place of newer growth, the lynx begins to move more cautiously. She frequently sits or hunches down to watch and listen.

Her attention fixes on a flicker of movement and a faint snapping sound ahead of her. At the edge of a clearing, a hare is nibbling birch twigs, his nervous glances darting in all directions.

The lynx begins to salivate. She has not made a kill since before the storm. She begins to creep slowly, silently, always staying in the cover of brush. She is only about as fast as the hare and has little endurance for running. Her best chance is to creep close, then leap from ambush.

About ten paces from the hare, she stops. If she comes any closer, she may reveal herself and scare away her prey.

The hare turns to nibble a winter bud. In a pounce, the lynx is halfway to him. The panicked hare streaks away. His feet, like hers, are large and well furred. He is even lighter on the snow than she is. Lynx and hare tear through the clearing, but after fifteen or twenty bounds, the lynx gives up the chase. The hare is too far ahead; her chance is lost. She will save her strength for another try.

The second hare does not escape. This time, hidden in a willow thicket, the lynx can almost grasp her prey before she pounces. In an instant, the hare hangs limp in the lynx's jaws.

The lynx drops the hare. She pulls out a patch of fur and tears open the hide with her teeth. Eating the flesh quiets her desperate hunger.

She beds down near the kill, licking the blood off her paws and muzzle, purring in contentment. Later, as the dawn twilight begins, she leaves to hunt once more before daybreak.

She was born three and a half years ago, in the late spring. That was a time of good hunting for the lynxes in her forest. Snowshoe hares, their primary food, were plentiful. Often a lynx had only to crouch low beside a hare trail and wait for one.

But the population of snowshoe hares is not constant. For about five years in a row, their numbers in a forest increase. At their peak, more than forty-five hundred hares may live in an area of one square mile (2.6 kilometers). But this area is not large enough to support so many hares. They begin to overgraze the plants they depend on for food, damaging or even killing them. Overcrowding may cause the hares to become aggressive toward one another, and disease may pass more quickly among the closely packed animals. Over the course of the next few years, the number of hares falls to a tiny fraction of what it had been at its peak.

During the lynx's first winter, hunting with her mother and littermates, she could not know that kills were coming less often than during the year before she was born.

In spring, she separated from her mother and found a territory of her own to hunt. As hares became harder to find, her territory grew larger. She had to travel farther each day to search out the few places where hares could still be found.

More and more, she had to stalk other prey. Sometimes she could surprise a ruffed grouse roosting under an evergreen tree, but grouse were not plentiful enough to make up for the lack of hares. She chased red squirrels, but they often escaped by running up tree trunks. In the warmer months, she caught voles, but in winter, they hid in snow tunnels. Hunting very small animals cost the lynx energy and gave her only a tiny meal in return, not enough to live on.

A large animal would provide the lynx with a great deal of food, but she was too small to bring down a full-grown moose or caribou by herself. She could bring down a calf, but calves were usually protected by mothers with powerful hooves.

Her skills worked best against snowshoe hares. Without a plentiful supply of hares to eat, she grew thin.

By the end of her second winter, hares had almost disappeared. In an area of forest where a thousand had been living only four years before, fewer than twenty remained. The next year was no better.

Many lynxes left the protection of the deep forest. They had always shrunk from contact with humans, but starvation made them reckless. Some of these nomads were shot in farmyards. Others were hit by cars. In the worst years of hunger, lynx kittens, born in the spring, did not survive to see winter. Young females who might have given birth in years of plenty did not have kittens at all.

A lynx might still determine the fate of a single snowshoe hare on a night's hunt. But the steady drop in the hare population led to the death of many lynxes. The predator could not survive without prey.

Then, last summer, snowshoe hares began to be more plentiful again. This winter, the lynx may kill three or more hares in a week, covering a smaller territory than during the lean hunting years.

If she kills more than one hare in a night, she does not need to gorge herself quickly after the second one. Sometimes her excitement in the hunt is stronger than her need to eat. She tosses the carcass up in the air, snatching it back each time. After eating part of it, she may "cache" the rest — cover it with dry leaves or snow — and come back to finish it later.

The blizzards of January and February deepen the snow and thicken the ice on lakes and rivers. The sun travels its low path in the sky from mid-morning to mid-afternoon. Some nights, the temperature falls to forty below zero.

For the lynx, it is a perfect time. Insulated in her winter fur, she trots confidently on the surface of snowdrifts many feet thick. This deep snow is her protection. She is a slow runner. On bare ground, wolves, wild dogs, or even a human could outrun her. But in deep snow, her enemies flounder while she outruns them all.

Deep snow also keeps a competitor out of her forest — the bobcat. If bobcats could live here, the lynx would be pushed out of her territory. Whenever lynxes compete with bobcats, their aggressive relatives, the lynxes are forced to retreat.

But bobcats cannot survive for long in deep snow country. Their small feet prevent them from treading on top of the snow to chase light-footed prey as lynxes can. They would soon starve.

Throughout the winter, the lynx shuns even the company of her own kind. Then in March, she feels the urge she has felt every spring — the urge to mate. The lynx has mated before, but in previous years she was too undernourished to produce kittens. This year, though, she is well fed.

Usually silent, she begins to mew and yowl, loudly and often. Sometimes she hears the wail of an answering male lynx. Her urine takes on a different smell. To a male lynx, this smell means that a female who may be ready to mate is nearby.

At the end of March, the lynx finds a mate. Before mating, the male and female yowl back and forth. Only when she is ready does the female lynx allow the male to approach her.

When they mate, the male grips the nape of the female's neck in his teeth. This causes her to become still, as it did when she was a kitten and her mother carried her by the scruff of the neck.

She and the male travel together for several days. During this time, they probably mate often. Then they separate. The male goes to look for another mate. The female returns to her solitary life. But she will not be alone for long. Healthy embryos have begun to develop inside her.

In early April, daytime temperatures bring melting, but night freezes all again. As patches of bare ground appear, the white snowshoe hares begin to grow patches of brown fur, staying as well disguised as they were against the winter snow. By summer they will be all brown. Because their coloration varies with the seasons, they are sometimes called varying hares.

The lynx, too, begins to shed her worn and ragged winter fur. Her summer coat will be shorter and browner, with darker markings. Like her gray winter coloring, it will make her difficult to see as long as she does not break cover.

The end of April brings a torrent of melting. Tiny rivulets become streams. Rivers tumble over their banks.

Water does not stop the lynx. Swimming with her head high out of the water, she can paddle across lakes two miles wide if she has to.

Birds that flew south for the winter return to nest. For the lynx, they are an additional source of food. Voles are easier to catch once again, now that they cannot hide in snow tunnels.

At the end of May, the lynx searches for a place within her territory for a safe den. In an area of old growth, where many dead trees have crashed down in storms, she finds a hollow log. There she gives birth to three kittens.

She licks each one clean and eats the afterbirth, the sack that surrounded each kitten in the womb. This helps nourish her, since she may go a day or more without hunting after the kittens' birth.

She purrs and mews to her newborns, nuzzling them to her belly. Eyes closed, ears folded, barely able to crawl, each kitten finds a nipple and begins to nurse. Without the warmth from their mother and one another, they would die of cold. Even in late spring, nights can be frosty.

Within two weeks after birth, the kittens' eyes open and their ears stand up. Their eyes will be deep blue for the first months of life. At the first sight of their littermates, the kittens make wobbly attempts to play-fight. They begin to explore their shelter, first crawling, then bounding. By the time they are a month old, they have begun to groom themselves.

The mother lynx never travels far from the den to hunt, but the kittens' best protection from predators is the jumble of downed trees and heavy undergrowth around them. When an owl or eagle swoops over the den or when a hungry wolverine is on the prowl, the kittens scramble for cover. Without it, they might not survive.

Summer brings an explosion of green to the forest. New growth flourishes in the many hours of sun and long twilights. For the kittens, the days are filled with rough and exciting play. They chase and pounce on anything that moves.

Summer is also the time for their first taste of meat. They are growing fast. They need meat now to stay healthy. This year, with the hare population increasing, their mother can kill often enough to feed herself and bring back prey to her kittens, too. At first, the kittens do not know how to get at the meat. They learn by watching their mother. Soon, they are hissing and snarling at one another, fighting for possession of the prey.

Other skills are learned by going on hunts with their mother. The ten-week-old kittens are eager for the chase, but on their own, they could not catch and kill prey. Their help is more accidental than deliberate. Romping through the brush, they sometimes flush out prey. It is their mother who runs it down — if the animal has not been sent bounding in the wrong direction.

With summer's end, the last of the migratory birds fly south again. Aspen leaves turn gold. Frost appears.

By the time October snows dot the forest with white, the fur of the snowshoe hares is changing again from brown to white. The lynxes are growing their winter coats.

The kittens hunt with their mother more often now, following her single file until they get to a place where hares are likely to be found. Then they fan out, taking zigzag paths about thirty paces apart. An animal stirred up by one of them may run into the path of one of the others.

Owls sometimes travel with the hunters, waiting for the chance to scoop up a fleeing animal before a lynx can grasp it.

    Success in the hunt comes more often as the kittens gain skill. By winter's end, chases result in captures more than half the time. A lynx hunting alone, even in a time of abundance, usually captures no more than four hares for every ten that are chased.

    The mother lynx probably still does most of the killing, but the time nears when the kittens will have to kill for themselves. Their mother's attachment to them is ending as her need to seek a new mate reawakens in March.

For a few months after they separate from their mother, the kittens will stay together. Then each will find a territory alone. Even though the hare population will continue to increase for a few years, their first year on their own will be a struggle, testing how well they have learned to stay hidden, crouch motionless for hours, and be silent when they stalk.

For their mother, the hunting will be good. Within her lifetime, she may never again face a time of starvation.

But other dangers lie in wait for her. Her forest is shrinking as human settlement comes closer. Someday the forest may be too small to sustain a population of lynxes. Or she may end her days in a trap, killed for her beautiful fur.

For now, she will roam her territory, unaware of these threats, a solitary hunter once more.

The Lynx: Vital Statistics

Latin name: *Lynx canadensis*

Origin of name: Possibly from the Greek "to see," referring to the lynx's keen sight

Similar species: In Europe and northern Asia, other lynx subspecies; in North America, the bobcat

Habitat: Mature forest for denning, young forest for hunting

Range: Forests of Canada, Alaska, the northern United States, and the Rocky Mountains south to Utah

Size: 15 to 25 pounds on average (7 to 11½ kilograms); 3 feet long (1 meter); males larger than females

Vocalizations: Mews, purrs, and wails like those of the domestic cat, but louder

Locomotion: Often leaps 6 to 10 feet (2 to 3 meters); excellent swimmer and climber

Food: Snowshoe hares, birds, small mammals; occasionally, deer and the young of moose and caribou

Mating: Mid-March to mid-April

Length of pregnancy: 60 to 65 days

Kittens born: Mid-May to mid-June

Size of litter: From 1 to 5, though usually 2 to 3

Status: Not listed as endangered at present, but populations in certain areas seriously damaged by overtrapping